ATREASURY OF CHRISTMAS POEMS

INTRODUCTION
BY
DAVID A. BOSSERT

Design and Layout by Nancy Levey-Bossert

Illustrations by Thomas Nast (1840-1902)
pages: 3, 4, 16, 31, 34, 42

Edited by Michele Orwin

Copy Edited by Diane Hodges

Set in Ornamental Versals by Måns Grebäck,
Bodoni 72 Oldstyle, New Press Eroded by Galdino Otten

Printed in Korea

First Edition, October 2019

ISBN: 978-1-7326020-1-4

Library of Congress Control Number: 20199422015

Visit www.theoldmillpress.com

A TREASURY OF CHRISTMAS POEMS

INTRODUCTION

Every year on Christmas Eve when I was young growing up on Long Island, my father would read some holiday-themed poems to my brother, sisters and me. It was a family tradition that carried on through high school and beyond. After Christmas Eve dinner, dad would call us all into the living room and he'd read "A Visit from St. Nicholas," better known as "Twas the Night Before Christmas," by Clement Clarke Moore. He read from a well-worn and faded copy of the book he'd kept from his childhood. Although his copy was tattered, he handled it with a gentle reverence he'd show to a rare first edition.

We were enthralled with the poem, as it signaled the impending delivery of presents. We had spent weeks going through the Sears Wish Book and dog-eared the pages with the toys we wanted. Our mother had marked pages with flannel shirts, corduroy pants and underwear– we ignored those. Our lists for Santa included only the most worthy and enviable playthings.

My father always read that poem in a very theatrical way, emphasizing certain words or pausing to make an exaggerated facial expression. Sometimes he even made side comments on some aspect of a passage, injecting a minor fact or some other obscure tidbit of information. His reading of the poem was always the highlight of our Christmas Eve.

By the time Dad finished reading, we were close to our bedtime. But right before heading to our bedrooms, we'd put out the milk and cookies for Santa, knowing they'd be devoured in mere hours. We were always a little suspicious of the interest Dad took in the selection of those cookies while grocery shopping days before.

When he was done, he'd usually tell us that Moore, the author, first published the poem anonymously. That it was published without attribution in the Troy, New York *Sentinel* on December 23, 1823, only because a friend of Moore's sent it into the paper. It wasn't until 1837 that Moore took credit for *A Visit from St. Nicholas* and in 1844, he included it in his own book of poems at the insistence of his children. I'm glad they did because Moore's poem was one of the first written descriptions of what Santa Claus looked like, which he based on a local Dutch handyman he knew. Moore was also inspired by Saint Nicholas of Myra, known for his secret gift-giving that gave rise to the current Santa Claus tradition many enjoy today.

This Christmas Eve tradition played out every year no matter where we were or what the weather was like. As we got older, we'd bemoan and complain about being read to but eventually acquiesced for no other reason than to not prolong the evening. We never got out of it and, looking back, I'm glad we didn't.

My dad continued to read these poems to his grandchildren until his death. Just as I will continue to read to my children and eventually my grandchildren.

"A Visit from St. Nicolas" wasn't the only poem that I recall from my childhood during the holidays. There were others, from well-known poets like D.H. Lawrence, Robert Frost and Henry Wadsworth Longfellow to lesser-known like Ella Rhoads Higginson, Eliza Cook and Joyce Kilmer, who was killed on a battlefield at Christmas in 1918 during WWI.

While there are other holiday poems, the ones included in this treasury have special meaning that I hope you will agree embody the spirit of the holiday season. Some will make you laugh, some may make you cry, others will invoke warm images of this joyous time with loved ones past and present.

To me it is the beauty of words that express feelings, emotions and thoughts. One poet called a poem "a thought, caught in the act of dawning." Another said a poem is "a means of bringing the wind in the grasses into the house." Still another stated, even more simply: "Poetry is a pheasant disappearing in the brush."[1] I think that if you ask many different people what poetry is, you'll get many different answers. That's because poetry affects each of us differently with its focus on words, how they sound, the textures, verse patterns, word choice and interpretations. All of that creates a verbal music—a rhythm, a cadence, a beat—that

---

(1) National Endowment for the Arts; What is Poetry? By Dan Rifenburgh

produces an emotional response in each of us, deep within our soul.

Every poem has a story to tell and some of those stories are so compelling that they have been made into films. *Howl* (2010) is about poet Allan Ginsberg and the writing of his seminal Beat Generation poem, *Howl*. The film was made as if it were a poem. *Beowulf* (2007), directed by Robert Zemeckis, is a film based on the epic Old English poem of the same name. Terry Gilliam, of Monty Python fame, directed *Jabberwocky* (1977) based on the nonsensical poem in Lewis Carroll's *Through the Looking-Glass*. I would be remiss of course if I didn't mention *Tim Burton's The Nightmare Before Christmas* (1993). Burton was a fan of the classic animated TV specials *Dr. Seuss' How the Grinch Stole Christmas!* and *Rudolph the Red-Nosed Reindeer* that aired every holiday season. His love of Halloween and Christmas inspired him to do his own original take on the poem *A Visit from St. Nicholas*. More than twenty-five years later *The Nightmare Before Christmas* has become a holiday viewing classic in its own right and it all started with a wonderful poem.

That was not the only take on *A Visit from St. Nicholas* from Disney. In 1933, Walt Disney Productions released the Silly Symphony short *The Night Before Christmas* based on Moore's poem. Since then, there have been various versions of the poem done over the years by Disney and other animation studios. Poetry is a source of inspiration within the cinematic and performing arts.

We all have our own traditions and create new ones as we grow from childhood into adulthood and start our own families. We adapt and reinvent those things that are personal to us and in doing so make lasting new memories for ourselves and loved ones. Traditions that grow from the wellspring of the Christmas holiday. A time of year that we break free of our daily routines and focus attention on visiting with friends and family. It is a time of year that brings us all together in a living room or by the warm glow of the hearth in the spirit of good tidings and joy.

When I first started to think about assembling this treasury of Christmas Poems, I thought about not only fond memories, but also about sharing the pleasure of the spoken word of poetry. Gathering these Christmas and holiday-themed poems in one volume so that they could be read silently or shared aloud. My hope is that you will find as much pleasure in reading these seasonal poems as I have over the years. Who knows, maybe you'll start your own holiday tradition of sharing them with your loved ones during the season of good will towards all with hope for peace on earth.

–Dave Bossert
Los Angeles, 2019

9

CHRISTMAS EVE

By Ella Rhoads Higginson

Straight thro' a fold of purple mist
The sun goes down—a crimson wheel—
And like an opal burns the sea
That once was cold as steel.

With pomp of purple, gold and red,
Thou wilt come back at morrow's dawn...
But thou can'st never bring, O Sun,
The Christmas that is gone!

Ella Rhoads Higginson (1862 – 1940) An American author and poet, she was born in Kansas and traveled by wagon train to Oregon where the family settled. She was the author of 6 books, hundreds of poems and short stories which drew international attention to the Pacific Northwest region of the United States.

A WINTER'S TALE

By D.H. Lawrence

Yesterday the fields were only grey with scattered snow,
And now the longest grass-leaves hardly emerge;
Yet her deep footsteps mark the snow, and go
On towards the pines at the hills' white verge.

I cannot see her, since the mist's white scarf
Obscures the dark wood and the dull orange sky;
But she's waiting, I know, impatient and cold, half
Sobs struggling into her frosty sigh.

Why does she come so promptly, when she must know
That she's only the nearer to the inevitable farewell;
The hill is steep, on the snow my steps are slow--
Why does she come, when she knows what I have to tell?

D. H. Lawrence (1885–1930) David Herbert Lawrence, novelist, short-story writer, poet, and essayist, was born in Eastwood, Nottinghamshire, England, on September 11, 1885. Though better known as a novelist, Lawrence's first-published works (in 1909) were poems, and his poetry, especially his evocations of the natural world, have since had a significant influence on many poets on both sides of the Atlantic.

STOPPING BY WOODS ON A SNOWY EVENING

By Robert Frost

Whose woods these are I think I know.
His house is in the village though;
He will not see me stopping here
To watch his woods fill up with snow.

My little horse must think it queer
To stop without a farmhouse near
Between the woods and frozen lake
The darkest evening of the year.

He gives his harness bells a shake
To ask if there is some mistake.
The only other sound's the sweep
Of easy wind and downy flake.

The woods are lovely, dark and deep,
But I have promises to keep,
And miles to go before I sleep,
And miles to go before I sleep.

Robert Frost (1874–1963) One of the most celebrated poets in America, Robert Frost was an author of searching and often dark meditations on universal themes and a quintessentially modern poet in his adherence to language as it is actually spoken, in the psychological complexity of his portraits, and in the degree to which his work is infused with layers of ambiguity and irony.

A VISIT FROM ST. NICHOLAS

('Twas the Night Before Christmas)
By Clement Clarke Moore

'Twas the night before Christmas, when all through the house
Not a creature was stirring, not even a mouse;
The stockings were hung by the chimney with care,
In hopes that St. Nicholas soon would be there;
The children were nestled all snug in their beds,
While visions of sugar-plums danced in their heads;
And mamma in her 'kerchief, and I in my cap,
Had just settled our brains for a long winter's nap,
When out on the lawn there arose such a clatter,
I sprang from the bed to see what was the matter.
Away to the window I flew like a flash,
Tore open the shutters and threw up the sash.
The moon on the breast of the new-fallen snow
Gave the luster of mid-day to objects below,
When, what to my wondering eyes should appear,
But a miniature sleigh, and eight tiny reindeer,
With a little old driver, so lively and quick,
I knew in a moment it must be St. Nick.
More rapid than eagles his coursers they came,
And he whistled, and shouted, and called them by name;

"Now, Dasher! now, Dancer! now, Prancer and Vixen!

On, Comet! on, Cupid! on, Donner and Blitzen!

To the top of the porch! to the top of the wall!

Now dash away! dash away! dash away all!"

As dry leaves that before the wild hurricane fly,

When they meet with an obstacle, mount to the sky;

So up to the house-top the coursers they flew,

With the sleigh full of Toys, and St. Nicholas too.

And then, in a twinkling, I heard on the roof

The prancing and pawing of each little hoof.

As I drew in my head, and was turning around,

Down the chimney St. Nicholas came with a bound.

He was dressed all in fur, from his head to his foot,

And his clothes were all tarnished with ashes and soot;

A bundle of Toys he had flung on his back,

And he looked like a peddler just opening his pack.

His eyes—how they twinkled! his dimples how merry!

His cheeks were like roses, his nose like a cherry!

His droll little mouth was drawn up like a bow

And the beard of his chin was as white as the snow;

The stump of a pipe he held tight in his teeth,

And the smoke it encircled his head like a wreath;

He had a broad face and a little round belly,

That shook when he laughed, like a bowlful of jelly.

He was chubby and plump, a right jolly old elf,

And I laughed when I saw him, in spite of myself;

A wink of his eye and a twist of his head,
Soon gave me to know I had nothing to dread;
He spoke not a word, but went straight to his work,
And filled all the stockings; then turned with a jerk,
And laying his finger aside of his nose,
And giving a nod, up the chimney he rose;
He sprang to his sleigh, to his team gave a whistle,
And away they all flew like the down of a thistle,
But I heard him exclaim, ere he drove out of sight,
"Happy Christmas to all, and to all a good-night."

Clement Clarke Moore (1779–1863) Born in New York City, Moore received a BA from Columbia College in 1798 and an MA in 1801. Moore was the author of many poems including the seminal Christmas poem "A Visit from St. Nicholas." Popularly known as "The Night before Christmas," it was first published anonymously in the Troy Sentinel in 1823. He taught at the General Theological Seminary in New York City from 1821 to 1850. He died on July 10, 1863, in Newport, Rhode Island.

CHRISTMAS BELLS

By Henry Wadsworth Longfellow

I heard the bells on Christmas Day
Their old, familiar carols play,
And wild and sweet
The words repeat
Of peace on earth, good-will to men!
And thought how, as the day had come,
The belfries of all Christendom
Had rolled along
The unbroken song
Of peace on earth, good-will to men!
Till, ringing, singing on its way
The world revolved from night to day,
A voice, a chime,
A chant sublime

Of peace on earth, good-will to men!
Then from each black, accursed mouth
The cannon thundered in the South,
And with the sound
The Carols drowned
Of peace on earth, good-will to men!
And in despair I bowed my head;
"There is no peace on earth," I said;
For hate is strong,
And mocks the song
Of peace on earth, good-will to men!
Then pealed the bells more loud and deep:
God is not dead; nor doth he sleep!
The Wrong shall fail,
The Right prevail,
With peace on earth, good-will to men!

Henry Wadsworth Longfellow (1807–1882) Known as one of the "Fireside Poets," he wrote lyrical poems about history, mythology, and legend that were popular and widely translated, making him the most famous American of his day.

CHRISTMAS TREES

By Robert Frost

A Christmas circular letter

The city had withdrawn into itself
And left at last the country to the country;
When between whirls of snow not come to lie
And whirls of foliage not yet laid, there drove
A stranger to our yard, who looked the city,
Yet did in country fashion in that there
He sat and waited till he drew us out,
A-buttoning coats, to ask him who he was.
He proved to be the city come again
To look for something it had left behind
And could not do without and keep its Christmas.
He asked if I would sell my Christmas trees;
My woods—the young fir balsams like a place
Where houses all are churches and have spires.
I hadn't thought of them as Christmas trees.
I doubt if I was tempted for a moment
To sell them off their feet to go in cars
And leave the slope behind the house all bare,

Where the sun shines now no warmer than the moon.
I'd hate to have them know it if I was.
Yet more I'd hate to hold my trees, except
As others hold theirs or refuse for them,
Beyond the time of profitable growth—
The trial by market everything must come to.
I dallied so much with the thought of selling.
Then whether from mistaken courtesy
And fear of seeming short of speech, or whether
From hope of hearing good of what was mine,
I said, "There aren't enough to be worth while."

"I could soon tell how many they would cut,
You let me look them over."

"You could look.
But don't expect I'm going to let you have them."
Pasture they spring in, some in clumps too close
That lop each other of boughs, but not a few
Quite solitary and having equal boughs
All round and round. The latter he nodded "Yes" to,
Or paused to say beneath some lovelier one,
With a buyer's moderation, "That would do."
I thought so too, but wasn't there to say so.
We climbed the pasture on the south, crossed over,

And came down on the north.

He said, "A thousand."

"A thousand Christmas trees!—at what apiece?"

He felt some need of softening that to me:
"A thousand trees would come to thirty dollars."

Then I was certain I had never meant
To let him have them. Never show surprise!
But thirty dollars seemed so small beside
The extent of pasture I should strip, three cents
(For that was all they figured out apiece)—
Three cents so small beside the dollar friends
I should be writing to within the hour
Would pay in cities for good trees like those,
Regular vestry-trees whole Sunday Schools
Could hang enough on to pick off enough.

A thousand Christmas trees I didn't know I had!
Worth three cents more to give away than sell,
As may be shown by a simple calculation.
Too bad I couldn't lay one in a letter.
I can't help wishing I could send you one,
In wishing you herewith a Merry Christmas.

Robert Frost (1874–1963) One of the most celebrated poets in America, Robert Frost was an author of searching and often dark meditations on universal themes and a quintessentially modern poet in his adherence to language as it is actually spoken, in the psychological complexity of his portraits, and in the degree to which his work is infused with layers of ambiguity and irony.

WARTIME CHRISTMAS

By Joyce Kilmer

Led by a star, a golden star,
The youngest star, an olden star,
Here the kings and the shepherds are,
A kneeling on the ground.
What did they come to the inn to see?
God in the Highest, and this is He,
A baby asleep on His mother's knee
And with her kisses crowned.

Now is the earth a dreary place,
A troubled place, a weary place.
Peace has hidden her lovely face
And turned in tears away.
Yet the sun, through the war-cloud, sees
Babies asleep on their mother's knees.
While there are love and home—and these—
There shall be Christmas Day.

Joyce Kilmer (1886–1918) was born on December 6, 1886, in New Brunswick, New Jersey. The author of *Main Street and Other Poems* (George H. Doran Company, 1917), he was killed while fighting in World War I.

THE CHRISTMAS HOLLY

By Eliza Cook

The holly! the holly! oh, twine it with bay—
Come give the holly a song;
For it helps to drive stern winter away,
With his garment so somber and long.
It peeps through the trees with its berries of red,
And its leaves of burnish'd green,
When the flowers and fruits have long been dead,
And not even the daisy is seen,
Then sing to the holly, the Christmas holly,
That hangs over peasant and king:
While we laugh and carouse 'neath its glitt'ring boughs,
To the Christmas holly we'll sing.

The gale may whistle, and frost may come,
To fetter the gurgling rill;
The woods may be bare, and the warblers dumb—
But the holly is beautiful still.
In the revel and light of princely halls,
The bright holly-branch is found;
And its shadow falls on the lowliest walls,

While the brimming horn goes round.
Then drink to the holly, &c.

The ivy lives long, but its home must be
Where graves and ruins are spread;
There's beauty about the cypress tree,
But it flourishes near the dead:
The laurel the warrior's brow may wreathe,
But it tells of tears and blood.
I sing the holly, and who can breathe
Aught of that that is not good?
Then sing to the holly, &c.

Eliza Cook (1818–1889) Was an English author and poet. She was an early feminist who believed in self-improvement through education, which made her hugely popular with the working class public in both England and America.

THE CHRISTMAS WREATH

By Anna de Brémont

Oh! Christmas wreath upon the wall,
Within thine ivied space
I see the years beyond recall,
Amid thy leaves I trace
The shadows of a happy past,
When all the world was bright,
And love its magic splendor cast
O'er morn and noon and night.

Oh! Christmas wreath upon the wall,
'Neath memory's tender spell
A wondrous charm doth o'er thee fall,
And round thy beauty dwell.
Thine ivy hath the satiny sheen
Of tresses I've caressed,
Thy holly's crimson gleam I've seen
On lips I oft have pressed.
Oh! Christmas wreath upon the wall,
A mist steals o'er my sight.

Dear hallow'd wreath, these tears are all
The pledge I now can plight
To those loved ones whose spirit eyes
Shine down the flight of time;
Around God's throne their voices rise
To swell the Christmas Chime!

Anna de Brémont (1849–1922) was an American journalist, novelist, poet and singer. She spent much of her life in England. A period in South Africa provided the material for some of her books.

THE ROAD NOT TAKEN

By Robert Frost

Two roads diverged in a yellow wood,
And sorry I could not travel both
And be one traveler, long I stood
And looked down one as far as I could
To where it bent in the undergrowth;

Then took the other, as just as fair,
And having perhaps the better claim,
Because it was grassy and wanted wear;
Though as for that the passing there
Had worn them really about the same,

And both that morning equally lay
In leaves no step had trodden black.
Oh, I kept the first for another day!
Yet knowing how way leads on to way,
I doubted if I should ever come back.

Two roads diverged in a yellow wood,
And sorry I could not travel both
And be one traveler, long I stood
And looked down one as far as I could
To where it bent in the undergrowth;

Then took the other, as just as fair,
And having perhaps the better claim,
Because it was grassy and wanted wear;
Though as for that the passing there
Had worn them really about the same,

And both that morning equally lay
In leaves no step had trodden black.
Oh, I kept the first for another day!
Yet knowing how way leads on to way,
I doubted if I should ever come back.
I shall be telling this with a sigh
Somewhere ages and ages hence:
Two roads diverged in a wood, and I—
I took the one less traveled by,
And that has made all the difference.

Robert Frost (1874–1963) One of the most celebrated poets in America, Robert Frost was an author of searching and often dark meditations on universal themes and a quintessentially modern poet in his adherence to language as it is actually spoken, in the psychological complexity of his portraits, and in the degree to which his work is infused with layers of ambiguity and irony.

A NATIVITY

By Rudyard Kipling

The Babe was laid in the Manger
Between the gentle kine—
All safe from cold and danger—
"But it was not so with mine,
　　　(With mine! With mine!)
"Is it well with the child, is it well?"
The waiting mother prayed.
"For I know not how he fell,
And I know not where he is laid."

A Star stood forth in Heaven;
The Watchers ran to see
The Sign of the Promise given—
"But there comes no sign to me.
　　　(To me! To me!)
"*My* child died in the dark.
Is it well with the child, is it well?
There was none to tend him or mark,
And I know not how he fell."

The Cross was raised on high;
The Mother grieved beside—
"But the Mother saw Him die
And took Him when He died.
(He died! He died!)
"Seemly and undefiled
His burial-place was made—
Is it well, is it well with the child?
For I know not where he is laid."

On the dawning of Easter Day
Comes Mary Magdalene;
But the Stone was rolled away,
And the Body was not within—
(Within! Within!)
"Ah, who will answer my word?"
The broken mother prayed.
"They have taken away my Lord,
And I know not where He is Laid."

"The Star stands forth in Heaven.
The watchers watch in vain
For Sign of the Promise given
Of peace on Earth again—
(Again! Again!)
"But I know for Whom he fell"—
The steadfast mother smiled,
"Is it well with the child—is it well?
It is well—it is well with the child!"

Joseph Rudyard Kipling (1865–1936) is best known for his novels *Captains Courageous, The Jungle Book* and *The Second Jungle Book* among others. He was born in Bombay, India to well off British family. His writing career began as a journalist and editor for the *Civil and Military Gazette* in Lahore, India. He published his first collection of poems in 1886 followed by his first collection of stories, *Plain Tales from the Hills,* in 1888. His ashes are buried in Westminster Abbey in London, England.

(little tree)

By E.E. Cummings

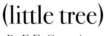

little tree
little silent Christmas tree
you are so little
you are more like a flower

who found you in the green forest
and were you very sorry to come away?
see   i will comfort you
because you smell so sweetly

i will kiss your cool bark
and hug you safe and tight
just as your mother would,
only don't be afraid

look   the spangles
that sleep all the year in a dark box
dreaming of being taken out and allowed to shine,
the balls the chains red and gold the fluffy threads,

put up your little arms
and i'll give them all to you to hold.
every finger shall have its ring
and there won't be a single place dark or unhappy

then when you're quite dressed
you'll stand in the window for everyone to see
and how they'll stare!
oh but you'll be very proud

and my little sister and i will take hands
and looking up at our beautiful tree
we'll dance and sing
"Noel Noel"

E. E. Cummings (1894 – 1962) is known for his radical experimentation with form, punctuation, spelling, and syntax; he abandoned traditional techniques and structures to create a new, highly idiosyncratic means of poetic expression.

HOLIDAYS

By Henry Wadsworth Longfellow

The holiest of all holidays are those
Kept by ourselves in silence and apart;
The secret anniversaries of the heart,
When the full river of feeling overflows;—
The happy days unclouded to their close;
The sudden joys that out of darkness start
As flames from ashes; swift desires that dart
Like swallows singing down each wind that blows!
White as the gleam of a receding sail,
White as a cloud that floats and fades in air,
White as the whitest lily on a stream,
These tender memories are;— a Fairy Tale
Of some enchanted land we know not where,
But lovely as a landscape in a dream.

Henry Wadsworth Longfellow (1807–1882) Known as one of the "Fireside Poets," he wrote lyrical poems about history, mythology, and legend that were popular and widely translated, making him the most famous American of his day.

Merry Christmas to all and to all a good night...

OLD SANTECLAUS

By Clement Clarke Moore

Old Santeclaus with much delight
His reindeer drives this frosty night,
O'er chimney-tops, and tracks of snow,
To bring his yearly gifts to you.

The steady friend of virtuous youth,
The friend of duty, and of truth,
Each Christmas eve he joys to come
Where love and peace have made their home.

Through many houses he has been,
And various beds and stockings seen;
Some, white as snow, and neatly mended,
Others, that seemed for pigs intended.
Where e'er I found good girls or boys,
That hated quarrels, strife and noise,
I left an apple, or a tart,
Or wooden gun, or painted cart.

To some I gave a pretty doll,
To some a peg-top, or a ball;
No crackers, cannons, squibs, or rockets,
To blow their eyes up, or their pockets.

No drums to stun their Mother's ear,
Nor swords to make their sisters fear;
But pretty books to store their mind
With knowledge of each various kind.

But where I found the children naughty,
In manners rude, in temper haughty,
Thankless to parents, liars, swearers,
Boxers, or cheats, or base tale-bearers,

I left a long, black, birchen rod,
Such as the dread command of God
Directs a Parent's hand to use
When virtue's path his sons refuse.

Clement Clarke Moore (1779–1863) Born in New York City, Moore received a BA from Columbia College in 1798 and an MA in 1801. Moore was the author of many poems including the seminal Christmas poem "A Visit from St. Nicholas." Popularly known as "The Night before Christmas," it was first published anonymously in the Troy Sentinel in 1823. He taught at the General Theological Seminary in New York City from 1821 to 1850. He died on July 10, 1863, in Newport, Rhode Island.

WALT DISNEY'S SCOTCH MIST

I wanted to include this note on the Scotch Mist because it always felt like a winter time beverage. The kind one might consume while sitting in front of a crackling fire on a snowy evening. The Scotch Mist, reported to be Walt Disney's favorite drink for imbibing, was made with Black and White scotch whisky, a lemon peel and served over crushed ice.

Walt's secretary Tommie Wilck would prepare his Scotch Mist drink at 5:00 PM each workday afternoon. The beverage was "mostly ice," Wilck said, in an interview years later. "He may have consumed a lot of liquid but I don't think he really got much liquor," she said.

The Black and White brand of Scotch Whiskey is made by the London based James Buchanan & Co Ltd. Over the years, the distillery went through a series of mergers and acquisitions and the brand is now owned by Diago plc, a multinational alcoholic beverages company headquartered in London. The Black and White blended Scotch whisky is only exported outside the U.K.

A Case of Christmas Cheer

May Your
Christmas be
a Happy One
And may the
New Year bring
You Contentment
and Prosperity
in overflowing
measure.